Mary Has a Baby

OK

EW TESTAMENT STORIES

LAMB BOOKS
Sight Reading

Mary Has a Baby

written by Tiffany Thomas
illustrated by Nikki Casassa

CFI • An imprint of Cedar Fort, Inc. • Springville, Utah

HARD WORDS:

angel, Elisabeth, Bethlehem

PARENT TIP: Choose one or two words for the child to read, with you reading the more difficult words. Each time you read through the story, have them read an additional one or two new words.

This is Mary.

Mary is
a good girl.
She loves God.

God picks Mary to be the mom of Jesus.

An angel comes
to see her.

Jesus is now in Mary's tummy.

Mary visits her cousin Elisabeth.

Elisabeth has a baby named John.

Mary marries Joseph.

They go to Bethlehem to pay taxe

There is no room at the inn.

Mary has Jesus in the stable.

The end.

ISBN 13: 978-1-4621-4403-7

Published by CFI, an imprint of Cedar Fort, Inc. • 2373 W. 700 S., Suite 100, Springville, UT 84663
Distributed by Cedar Fort, Inc., www.cedarfort.com

Library of Congress Control Number: 2022950658

Cover design and interior layout design by Shawnda T. Craig

Printed in China • Printed on acid-free paper
10 9 8 7 6 5 4 3 2 1

HELP your child read while also learning about the stories from the New Testament. Build your child's confidence in reading with the entire LAMB BOOKS series as they progress through each book!

MORE BOOK SETS AVAILABLE IN THE LAMB BOOKS SERIES

OLD TESTAMENT STORIES

FIRST GRADE READING LEVEL
APPEALS TO PRE-K – FIRST GRADE

See cedarfort.com for more uplifting children's books.

CFI
CEDAR FORT
WWW.CEDARFORT.COM
WWW.AUTHORTIFFANYTHOMAS.COM

...he Shepherds and the Wise Men

LAMB BOOKS

Sight Reading

...W TESTAMENT STORIES

The Shepherds and the Wise Men

written by Tiffany Thomas
illustrated by Nikki Casassa

CFI • An imprint of Cedar Fort, Inc. • Springville, Utah

HARD WORDS:

shepherd, field, herod

PARENT TIP: Have the child use a finger, craft stick, twig, or other item to point to each word as they read.

These are the shepherds.

They are in the fields
with their sheep.

The angels say Jesus is born.

The shepherds see Jesus.

These are the wise men.

They see the new star.

The wise men follow the star a long way.

They ask Herod where the king of the Jews is.

The wise men find Jesus and give Him gifts.

An angel tells them
Herod is bad.

The wise men
go another way.

The end.

ISBN 13: 978-1-4621-4403-7

Published by CFI, an imprint of Cedar Fort, Inc. • 2373 W. 700 S., Suite 100, Springville, UT 84663
Distributed by Cedar Fort, Inc., www.cedarfort.com

Library of Congress Control Number: 2022950658

Cover design and interior layout design by Shawnda T. Craig

Printed in China • Printed on acid-free paper
10 9 8 7 6 5 4 3 2 1

HELP your child read while also learning about the stories from the New Testament. Build your child's confidence in reading with the entire LAMB BOOKS series as they progress through each book!

MORE BOOK SETS AVAILABLE IN THE LAMB BOOKS SERIES

OLD TESTAMENT STORIES

FIRST GRADE READING LEVEL
APPEALS TO PRE-K – FIRST GRADE

See cedarfort.com for more uplifting children's books.

Jesus Grows Up

EW TESTAMENT STORIES

LAMB BOOKS
Sight Reading

Jesus Grows Up

written by Tiffany Thomas
illustrated by Nikki Casassa

CFI • An imprint of Cedar Fort, Inc. • Springville, Utah

HARD WORDS:
temple, teaches, grown

PARENT TIP: If you or your child begin to feel frustrated about reading, take a break. Or stop and say a prayer.

Jesus was a baby.

Now He is getting bigger.

Joseph works with wood.

He teaches Jesus how to work with wood too.

Now Jesus is 12 years old.

Mary, Joseph, and Jesus go to the temple.

Mary thinks Jesus is lost.
She is scared.

Jesus is at the temple.

Jesus teaches the grown men about God.

They think Jesus is very smart.

Mary finds Jesus and hugs Him.

The end.

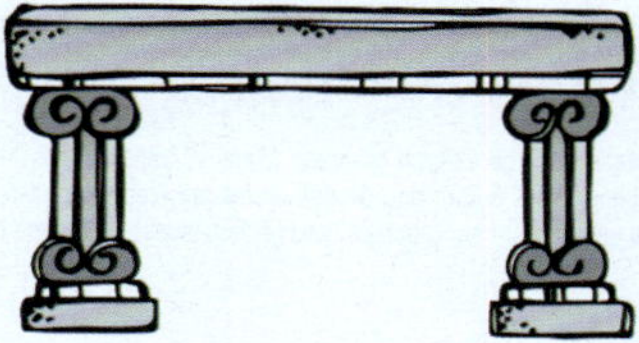

ISBN 13: 978-1-4621-4403-7

Published by CFI, an imprint of Cedar Fort, Inc. • 2373 W. 700 S., Suite 100, Springville, UT 84663
Distributed by Cedar Fort, Inc., www.cedarfort.com

Library of Congress Control Number: 2022950658

Cover design and interior layout design by Shawnda T. Craig

Printed in China • Printed on acid-free paper
10 9 8 7 6 5 4 3 2 1

HELP your child read while also learning about the stories from the New Testament. Build your child's confidence in reading with the entire LAMB BOOKS series as they progress through each book!

MORE BOOK SETS AVAILABLE IN THE LAMB BOOKS SERIES

OLD TESTAMENT STORIES

FIRST GRADE READING LEVEL
APPEALS TO PRE-K – FIRST GRADE

See cedarfort.com for more uplifting children's books.

CFI
CEDAR FORT
WWW.CEDARFORT.COM
WWW.AUTHORTIFFANYTHOMAS.COM

John Baptizes Jesus

EW TESTAMENT STORIES

LAMB
BOOKS
Sight Reading

John Baptizes Jesus

written by Tiffany Thomas
illustrated by Nikki Casassa

CFI • An imprint of Cedar Fort, Inc. • Springville, Utah

HARD WORDS:
Baptist, cousin, perfect

PARENT TIP: Reading the same books over and over again helps increase fluency and speed.

This is John the Baptist.

He is the cousin of Jesus.

Jesus has
grown up.
He is perfect.

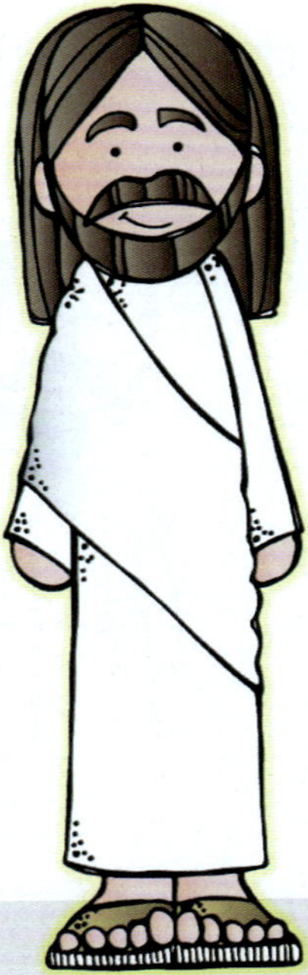

He does not sin
or do bad.

He wants to be baptized.

Jesus goes to John the Baptist.

John says, "No, you are perfect."

Jesus says He wants to obey.

John baptizes Jesus
in the river.

The Holy Ghost sends a dove.

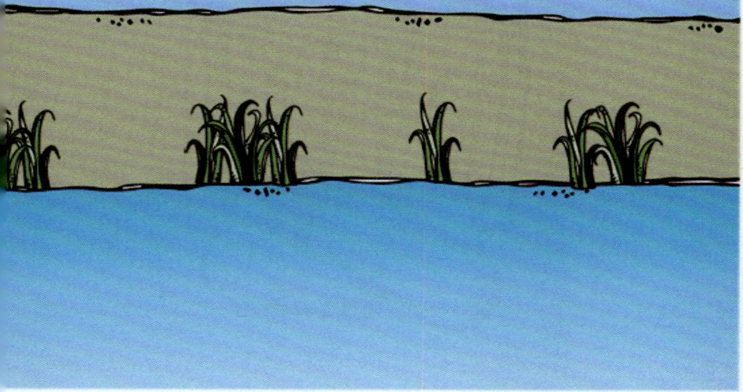

God is proud of Jesus.

The end.

ISBN 13: 978-1-4621-4403-7

Published by CFI, an imprint of Cedar Fort, Inc. • 2373 W. 700 S., Suite 100, Springville, UT 84663
Distributed by Cedar Fort, Inc., www.cedarfort.com

Library of Congress Control Number: 2022950658

Cover design and interior layout design by Shawnda T. Craig

Printed in China • Printed on acid-free paper
10 9 8 7 6 5 4 3 2 1

HELP your child read while also learning about the stories from the New Testament. Build your child's confidence in reading with the entire LAMB BOOKS series as they progress through each book!

MORE BOOK SETS AVAILABLE IN THE LAMB BOOKS SERIES

OLD TESTAMENT STORIES

FIRST GRADE READING LEVEL
APPEALS TO PRE-K – FIRST GRADE

See cedarfort.com for more uplifting children's books.

EBOOK

CFI
AN IMPRINT OF CEDAR FORT, INC.

CEDAR FORT
Publishing & Media

WWW.CEDARFORT.COM
WWW.AUTHORTIFFANYTHOMAS.COM

Satan Tempts Jesus

EW TESTAMENT STORIES

LAMB
BOOKS
Sight Reading

Satan Tempts Jesus

written by Tiffany Thomas
illustrated by Nikki Casassa

CFI • An imprint of Cedar Fort, Inc. • Springville, Utah

HARD WORDS:
desert, tempt, Satan

PARENT TIP: Repetition is the key to learning and remembering new sight words. Your child may need to see a new sight word many times before they recognize and remember it.

Jesus goes to
the desert.

He fasts for forty days. He is very hungry.

Satan comes and tempts Jesus.

Satan tells
Jesus to turn
the rocks
to bread.

Jesus does not listen.

Satan put Jesus on
the top of the temple.

Satan tells Jesus to jump off.
Jesus says no.

Satan took Jesus
to the top of
a mountain.

Satan says he will make Jesus ric

Jesus will
not bow
down to
Satan.

Satan is mad and goes away.

The end.

ISBN 13: 978-1-4621-4403-7

Published by CFI, an imprint of Cedar Fort, Inc. • 2373 W. 700 S., Suite 100, Springville, UT 84663
Distributed by Cedar Fort, Inc., www.cedarfort.com

Library of Congress Control Number: 2022950658

Cover design and interior layout design by Shawnda T. Craig

Printed in China • Printed on acid-free paper
10 9 8 7 6 5 4 3 2 1

HELP your child read while also learning about the stories from the New Testament. Build your child's confidence in reading with the entire LAMB BOOKS series as they progress through each book!

MORE BOOK SETS AVAILABLE IN THE LAMB BOOKS SERIES

OLD TESTAMENT STORIES

FIRST GRADE READING LEVEL
APPEALS TO PRE-K – FIRST GRADE

See cedarfort.com for more uplifting children's books.

EBOOK

CFI
AN IMPRINT OF CEDAR FORT, INC.

CEDAR FORT
Publishing & Media

WWW.CEDARFORT.COM
WWW.AUTHORTIFFANYTHOMAS.COM

LAM
BOO
Sight Re

The Woman at the Well

LAMB BOOKS

Sight Reading

ƎW TESTAMENT STORIES

The Woman at the Well

written by Tiffany Thomas
illustrated by Nikki Casassa

CFI • An imprint of Cedar Fort, Inc. • Springville, Utah

HARD WORDS:

Samaria, people, believe

PARENT TIP: Have your child read out loud, even if they can read all of the words by themselves.

Jesus travels to Samaria.

The Jews did not like Samaritans.

There is a woman at the well.

She is a Samaritan.

Jesus asks her for
a drink of water.

She is surprised He talked to her.

He tells her He
could give her water.

With His water she won't be thirsty again.

She asks if He is the Savior.
He says yes.

She goes to the town
and tells all the people.

Many people come and believe Him, too.

The end.

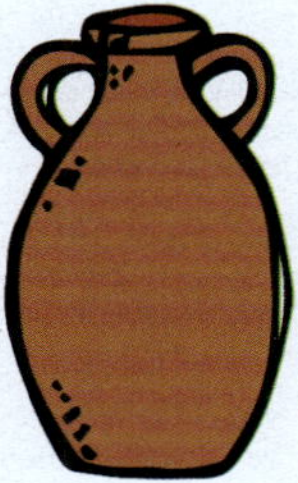

ISBN 13: 978-1-4621-4403-7

Published by CFI, an imprint of Cedar Fort, Inc. • 2373 W. 700 S., Suite 100, Springville, UT 84663
Distributed by Cedar Fort, Inc., www.cedarfort.com

Library of Congress Control Number: 2022950658

Cover design and interior layout design by Shawnda T. Craig

Printed in China • Printed on acid-free paper
10 9 8 7 6 5 4 3 2 1

HELP your child read while also learning about the stories from the New Testament. Build your child's confidence in reading with the entire LAMB BOOKS series as they progress through each book!

MORE BOOK SETS AVAILABLE IN THE LAMB BOOKS SERIES

OLD TESTAMENT STORIES

FIRST GRADE READING LEVEL
APPEALS TO PRE-K – FIRST GRADE

See cedarfort.com for more uplifting children's books.

EBOOK

CFI
AN IMPRINT OF CEDAR FORT, INC.

CEDAR FORT Publishing & Media

WWW.CEDARFORT.COM
WWW.AUTHORTIFFANYTHOMAS.COM

The Winds and Waves

N TESTAMENT STORIES

LAMB BOOKS
Sight Reading

The Winds and Waves

written by Tiffany Thomas
illustrated by Nikki Casassa

CFI • An imprint of Cedar Fort, Inc. • Springville, Utah

HARD WORDS:

Apostle, scared, peace

PARENT TIP: When your child is stuck o a word, do not say the word for them. Coun to five in your head, and then share a strateg to figure it out. (Look at the picture, sound i out, etc.)

Jesus is on the sea
with His Apostles.

He is very tired
from helping people.

Jesus falls asleep
on the boat.

The wind begins to
blow very hard.

There are big waves.

The boat begins to fill with water.

The Apostles are scared it will sink.

They wake up Jesus.

Jesus tells the winds
and the waves to stop.

"Peace, be still."
The sea is now calm.

Jesus says the Apostles need more faith.

The end.

ISBN 13: 978-1-4621-4403-7

Published by CFI, an imprint of Cedar Fort, Inc. • 2373 W. 700 S., Suite 100, Springville, UT 84663
Distributed by Cedar Fort, Inc., www.cedarfort.com

Library of Congress Control Number: 2022950658

Cover design and interior layout design by Shawnda T. Craig

Printed in China • Printed on acid-free paper
10 9 8 7 6 5 4 3 2 1

HELP your child read while also learning about the stories from the New Testament. Build your child's confidence in reading with the entire LAMB BOOKS series as they progress through each book!

MORE BOOK SETS AVAILABLE IN THE LAMB BOOKS SERIES

OLD TESTAMENT STORIES

FIRST GRADE READING LEVEL
APPEALS TO PRE-K – FIRST GRADE

See cedarfort.com for more uplifting children's books.

EBOOK

CFI
AN IMPRINT OF CEDAR FORT, INC.

CEDAR FORT Publishing & Media

WWW.CEDARFORT.COM
WWW.AUTHORTIFFANYTHOMAS.COM

The Man Who Can't Walk

LAMB
BOOKS
Sight Reading

N TESTAMENT STORIES

The Man Who Can't Walk

written by Tiffany Thomas
illustrated by Nikki Casassa

CFI • An imprint of Cedar Fort, Inc. • Springville, Utah

HARD WORDS:

house, lowered, Pharisee

PARENT TIP: Check for understanding After a few pages, ask the child what has happened in the story so far.

Jesus is teaching a group of people in a house.

Some men carry a man on a bed.
The man can't walk.

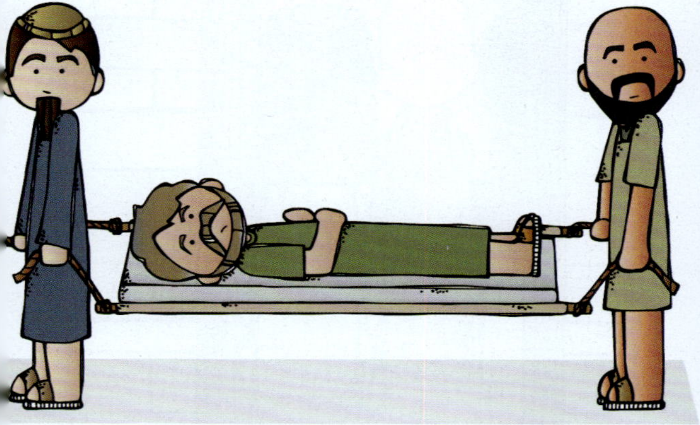

The crowd is too big.

They cannot get the bed into the house.

The men take their friend to the roof.

They take off part of the roof.

The man on the bed is lowered dow

esus forgives the man of his sins.

The Pharisees are mad.

Jesus tells the
man to pick up
his bed and walk.

The man stands up healed.

The end.

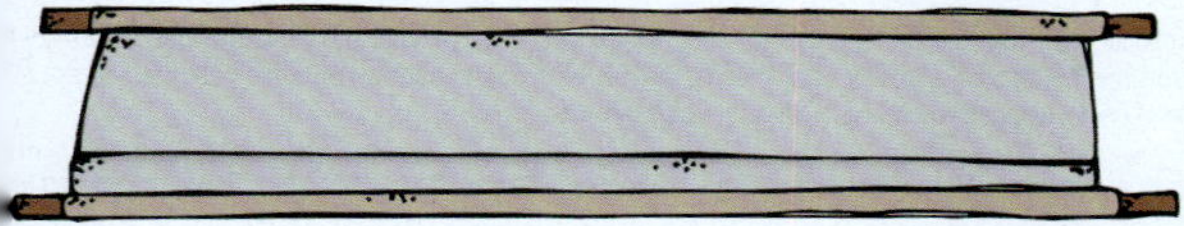

ISBN 13: 978-1-4621-4403-7

Published by CFI, an imprint of Cedar Fort, Inc. • 2373 W. 700 S., Suite 100, Springville, UT 84663
Distributed by Cedar Fort, Inc., www.cedarfort.com

Library of Congress Control Number: 2022950658

Cover design and interior layout design by Shawnda T. Craig

Printed in China • Printed on acid-free paper
10 9 8 7 6 5 4 3 2 1

HELP your child read while also learning about the stories from the New Testament. Build your child's confidence in reading with the entire LAMB BOOKS series as they progress through each book!

MORE BOOK SETS AVAILABLE IN THE LAMB BOOKS SERIES

OLD TESTAMENT STORIES

FIRST GRADE READING LEVEL
APPEALS TO PRE-K – FIRST GRADE

See cedarfort.com for more uplifting children's books.

EBOOK
CFI
AN IMPRINT OF CEDAR FORT, INC.
CEDAR FORT
Publishing & Media
WWW.CEDARFORT.COM
WWW.AUTHORTIFFANYTHOMAS.COM

The Girl Is Alive Again

LAMB BOOKS

Sight Reading

TESTAMENT STORIES

The Girl Is Alive Again

written by Tiffany Thomas
illustrated by Nikki Casassa

CFI • An imprint of Cedar Fort, Inc. • Springville, Utah

HARD WORDS:

Jairus, daughter, laugh

PARENT TIP: Find a comfortable place t do your reading, like the couch, the bed, or soft chair.

This is Jairus.
He is a leader of Jews.

His daughter is twelve years old.

She is very sick,
and she may die.

Jairus asks Jesus to come and heal her.

Jesus comes, but a man tells Jairus it is too late.

Jesus tells Jairus to have faith.

The people in the house
are sad and crying.

Jesus says she is only asleep.
The people laugh at Him.

Jesus tells them to leave.

He tells the girl to get up.

She comes back to life.

The end.

ISBN 13: 978-1-4621-4403-7

Published by CFI, an imprint of Cedar Fort, Inc. • 2373 W. 700 S., Suite 100, Springville, UT 84663
Distributed by Cedar Fort, Inc., www.cedarfort.com

Library of Congress Control Number: 2022950658

Cover design and interior layout design by Shawnda T. Craig

Printed in China • Printed on acid-free paper
10 9 8 7 6 5 4 3 2 1

HELP your child read while also learning about the stories from the New Testament. Build your child's confidence in reading with the entire LAMB BOOKS series as they progress through each book!

MORE BOOK SETS AVAILABLE IN THE LAMB BOOKS SERIES

OLD TESTAMENT STORIES

FIRST GRADE READING LEVEL
APPEALS TO PRE-K – FIRST GRADE

See cedarfort.com for more uplifting children's books.

ALSO AVAILABLE AS AN EBOOK

CFI AN IMPRINT OF CEDAR FORT, INC.

CEDAR FORT Publishing & Media

WWW.CEDARFORT.COM
WWW.AUTHORTIFFANYTHOMAS.COM

A Woman Touches Jesus's Robe

LAMB BOOKS
Sight Reading

NEW TESTAMENT STORIES

A Woman Touches Jesus's Robe

written by Tiffany Thomas
illustrated by Nikki Casassa

CFI • An imprint of Cedar Fort, Inc. • Springville, Utah

HARD WORDS:
touch, healed, faith

PARENT TIP: At the end of the story, have your child act out what was read.

This woman
is sick.

She has been sick
for a very long time.

The doctors cannot help her.

She knows Jesus is coming.

She wants to touch His robe.

She knows it
will heal her.

The woman touches His robe.

Jesus asks, "Who touched me?"

There are lots of people, and no one knows.

The woman says she touched Him.

He tells her that her faith healed her.

The end.

ISBN 13: 978-1-4621-4403-7

Published by CFI, an imprint of Cedar Fort, Inc. • 2373 W. 700 S., Suite 100, Springville, UT 84663
Distributed by Cedar Fort, Inc., www.cedarfort.com

Library of Congress Control Number: 2022950658

Cover design and interior layout design by Shawnda T. Craig

Printed in China • Printed on acid-free paper
10 9 8 7 6 5 4 3 2 1

HELP your child read while also learning about the stories from the New Testament. Build your child's confidence in reading with the entire LAMB BOOKS series as they progress through each book!

MORE BOOK SETS AVAILABLE IN THE LAMB BOOKS SERIES

OLD TESTAMENT STORIES

FIRST GRADE READING LEVEL
APPEALS TO PRE-K – FIRST GRADE

See cedarfort.com for more uplifting children's books.

EBOOK

CFI
AN IMPRINT OF CEDAR FORT, INC.

CEDAR FORT Publishing & Media

WWW.CEDARFORT.COM
WWW.AUTHORTIFFANYTHOMAS.COM

Jesus Forgives a Woman

TESTAMENT STORIES

LAMB BOOKS

Sight Reading

Jesus Forgives a Woman

written by Tiffany Thomas
illustrated by Nikki Casassa

CFI • An imprint of Cedar Fort, Inc. • Springville, Utah

HARD WORDS:

something, sinner, hair

PARENT TIP: Give frequent praise especially when they keep working on a difficult word.

Jesus is eating dinner
at a Pharisee's house.

A woman hears He is there.

She has done bad things.

But she still loves Jesus.

She wants to do something nice for Him.

She washes Jesus's feet with her tears.

She dries His feet with her hair.

She kisses His feet and puts sweet oil on them.

The Pharisee is not happy because the woman is a sinner.

Jesus says she loves Him.

Jesus forgives the woman's sins

The end.

ISBN 13: 978-1-4621-4403-7

Published by CFI, an imprint of Cedar Fort, Inc. • 2373 W. 700 S., Suite 100, Springville, UT 84663
Distributed by Cedar Fort, Inc., www.cedarfort.com

Library of Congress Control Number: 2022950658

Cover design and interior layout design by Shawnda T. Craig

Printed in China • Printed on acid-free paper
10 9 8 7 6 5 4 3 2 1

HELP your child read while also learning about the stories from the New Testament. Build your child's confidence in reading with the entire LAMB BOOKS series as they progress through each book!

MORE BOOK SETS AVAILABLE IN THE LAMB BOOKS SERIES

OLD TESTAMENT STORIES

FIRST GRADE READING LEVEL
APPEALS TO PRE-K – FIRST GRADE

See cedarfort.com for more uplifting children's books.

ALSO AVAILABLE AS AN EBOOK

CFI
AN IMPRINT OF CEDAR FORT, INC.

CEDAR FORT
Publishing & Media

WWW.CEDARFORT.COM
WWW.AUTHORTIFFANYTHOMAS.COM

esus Feeds Lots of People

W TESTAMENT STORIES

LAMB BOOKS
Sight Reading

Jesus Feeds Lots of People

written by Tiffany Thomas
illustrated by Nikki Casassa

CFI • An imprint of Cedar Fort, Inc. • Springville, Utah

HARD WORDS:

follow, loaves, blesses

PARENT TIP: Encourage your child to read aloud to other people, such as siblings and grandparents.

Some men tell Jesus that his cousin John has died.

Jesus is
very sad.
He loved John.

Jesus goes to the sea to be alone

More than 5,000 people follow Him.

They want Jesus to teach them.

Jesus teaches them all day long.

It was time to eat,
but no one had food.

A boy has five loaves of bread and two fish.

Jesus blesses the food and breaks it.

The Apostles hand out the food.

There is enough to feed all the people, plus extra.

The end.

ISBN 13: 978-1-4621-4403-7

Published by CFI, an imprint of Cedar Fort, Inc. • 2373 W. 700 S., Suite 100, Springville, UT 84663
Distributed by Cedar Fort, Inc., www.cedarfort.com

Library of Congress Control Number: 2022950658

Cover design and interior layout design by Shawnda T. Craig

Printed in China • Printed on acid-free paper
10 9 8 7 6 5 4 3 2 1

HELP your child read while also learning about the stories from the New Testament. Build your child's confidence in reading with the entire LAMB BOOKS series as they progress through each book!

MORE BOOK SETS AVAILABLE IN THE LAMB BOOKS SERIES

OLD TESTAMENT STORIES

FIRST GRADE READING LEVEL
APPEALS TO PRE-K – FIRST GRADE

See cedarfort.com for more uplifting children's books.

ALSO AVAILABLE AS AN EBOOK

CFI
AN IMPRINT OF CEDAR FORT, INC.

CEDAR FORT Publishing & Media

WWW.CEDARFORT.COM
WWW.AUTHORTIFFANYTHOMAS.COM

Jesus Walks on Water

LAMB BOOKS

Sight Reading

N TESTAMENT STORIES

Jesus Walks on Water

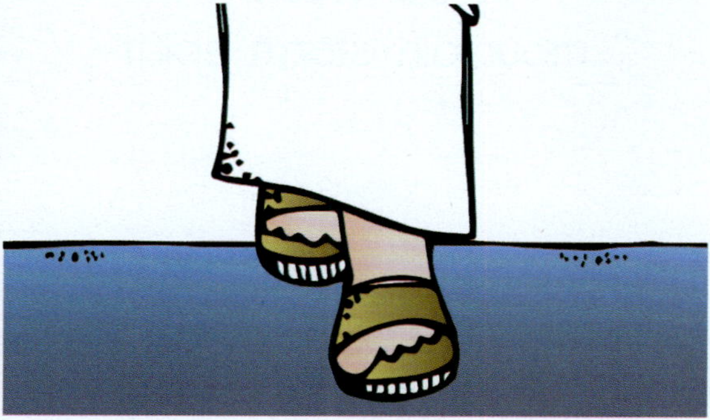

written by Tiffany Thomas
illustrated by Nikki Casassa

CFI • An imprint of Cedar Fort, Inc. • Springville, Utah

HARD WORDS:
mountain, storm, spirit

PARENT TIP: If the child feels overwhelmed cover the following words so they only see one word. Do not cover the pictures.

Jesus goes up on
a mountain to pray.

The Apostles are on a boat at night.

A storm comes.
They are scared.

Jesus walks on the water to the boat.

The Apostles think He is a spirit.

Jesus says, "It is I. Be not afraid."

Peter tries to walk to Jesus.

He gets scared of the waves and starts to sink.

Jesus grabs his hand
and says to have more faith.

When they reach the boat, the storm stops.

They know Jesus is the Son of Go

The end.

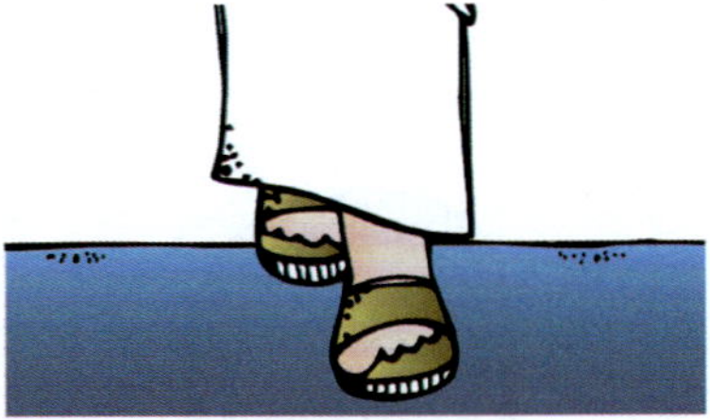

ISBN 13: 978-1-4621-4403-7

Published by CFI, an imprint of Cedar Fort, Inc. • 2373 W. 700 S., Suite 100, Springville, UT 84663
Distributed by Cedar Fort, Inc., www.cedarfort.com

Library of Congress Control Number: 2022950658

Cover design and interior layout design by Shawnda T. Craig

Printed in China • Printed on acid-free paper
10 9 8 7 6 5 4 3 2 1

HELP your child read while also learning about the stories from the New Testament. Build your child's confidence in reading with the entire LAMB BOOKS series as they progress through each book!

MORE BOOK SETS AVAILABLE IN THE LAMB BOOKS SERIES

OLD TESTAMENT STORIES

FIRST GRADE READING LEVEL
APPEALS TO PRE-K – FIRST GRADE

See cedarfort.com for more uplifting children's books.

EBOOK

CFI
AN IMPRINT OF CEDAR FORT, INC.

CEDAR FORT
Publishing & Media

WWW.CEDARFORT.COM
WWW.AUTHORTIFFANYTHOMAS.COM

LAM
BOOK
Sight Read

The Good Samaritan

EW TESTAMENT STORIES

LAMB BOOKS
Sight Reading

The Good Samaritan

written by Tiffany Thomas
illustrated by Nikki Casassa

CFI • An imprint of Cedar Fort, Inc. • Springville, Utah

HARD WORDS:

should, samaritan, enemies

PARENT TIP: Have a special celebration the first time a child reads an entire book without help.

Jesus tells a story to teach who we should help.

A Jew goes on a trip.

Bad men rob and hurt the Jew.

The Jew is left on
the side of the road.

People passed by him two times, but no one helped.

A Samaritan comes by.

Jews and Samaritans fight a lot.

The Samaritan took the man to an inn.

He pays the inn keeper
to care for the man.

Jesus says the Samaritan was the better man.

We should help everyone, even enemies.

The end.

ISBN 13: 978-1-4621-4403-7

Published by CFI, an imprint of Cedar Fort, Inc. • 2373 W. 700 S., Suite 100, Springville, UT 84663
Distributed by Cedar Fort, Inc., www.cedarfort.com

Library of Congress Control Number: 2022950658

Cover design and interior layout design by Shawnda T. Craig

Printed in China • Printed on acid-free paper
10 9 8 7 6 5 4 3 2 1

HELP your child read while also learning about the stories from the New Testament. Build your child's confidence in reading with the entire LAMB BOOKS series as they progress through each book!

MORE BOOK SETS AVAILABLE IN THE LAMB BOOKS SERIES

OLD TESTAMENT STORIES

FIRST GRADE READING LEVEL
APPEALS TO PRE-K – FIRST GRADE

See cedarfort.com for more uplifting children's books.

EBOOK

CFI
AN IMPRINT OF CEDAR FORT, INC.

CEDAR FORT
Publishing & Media

WWW.CEDARFORT.COM
WWW.AUTHORTIFFANYTHOMAS.COM

The Lost Son

LAMB BOOKS
Sight Reading

W TESTAMENT STORIES

The Lost Son

written by Tiffany Thomas
illustrated by Nikki Casassa

CFI • An imprint of Cedar Fort, Inc. • Springville, Utah

HARD WORDS:

money, waste, forgive

PARENT TIP: Do not push a child to rea

so much that they develop reading fatigue.

Jesus tells a story about
a rich man with two sons.

One of the sons helps
his dad and works hard.

The other son asks for his money

The son takes the money and goes away.

The son wastes the money on bad things.

The son has no money now.
He is hungry.

He gets a job feeding pigs.
He eats their food.

He chooses to go back home.

The dad sees the son and hugs him.

There is a party.
The first son is mad.

The dad tells the son
to forgive and be happy.

The end.

ISBN 13: 978-1-4621-4403-7

Published by CFI, an imprint of Cedar Fort, Inc. • 2373 W. 700 S., Suite 100, Springville, UT 84663
Distributed by Cedar Fort, Inc., www.cedarfort.com

Library of Congress Control Number: 2022950658

Cover design and interior layout design by Shawnda T. Craig

Printed in China • Printed on acid-free paper
10 9 8 7 6 5 4 3 2 1

HELP your child read while also learning about the stories from the New Testament. Build your child's confidence in reading with the entire LAMB BOOKS series as they progress through each book!

MORE BOOK SETS AVAILABLE IN THE LAMB BOOKS SERIES

OLD TESTAMENT STORIES

FIRST GRADE READING LEVEL
APPEALS TO PRE-K – FIRST GRADE

See cedarfort.com for more uplifting children's books.

EBOOK
CFI
AN IMPRINT OF CEDAR FORT, INC.
CEDAR FORT Publishing & Media
WWW.CEDARFORT.COM
WWW.AUTHORTIFFANYTHOMAS.COM

Jesus Heals Ten Lepers

W TESTAMENT STORIES

LAMB
BOOKS
Sight Reading

Jesus Heals Ten Lepers

written by Tiffany Thomas
illustrated by Nikki Casassa

CFI • An imprint of Cedar Fort, Inc. • Springville, Utah

HARD WORDS:

leper, thank, priest

PARENT TIP: If the child struggles with blending consonants, try saying other words with those same blends. Example: brings, bread, brake, brown.

These ten men are sick.

Their skin has sores.
They are lepers.

Doctors cannot help lepers.

No one wants to be by them and get sick, too.

The lepers ask Jesus to heal them

Jesus tells the lepers
to go to the priest.

The ten men obey Jesus.

n their way, the lepers are healed!

Only one comes back
to say thank you.

Jesus asks where the other nine are.

They did not come to thank Him.

The end.

ISBN 13: 978-1-4621-4403-7

Published by CFI, an imprint of Cedar Fort, Inc. • 2373 W. 700 S., Suite 100, Springville, UT 84663
Distributed by Cedar Fort, Inc., www.cedarfort.com

Library of Congress Control Number: 2022950658

Cover design and interior layout design by Shawnda T. Craig

Printed in China • Printed on acid-free paper
10 9 8 7 6 5 4 3 2 1

HELP your child read while also learning about the stories from the New Testament. Build your child's confidence in reading with the entire LAMB BOOKS series as they progress through each book!

MORE BOOK SETS AVAILABLE IN THE LAMB BOOKS SERIES

OLD TESTAMENT STORIES

FIRST GRADE READING LEVEL
APPEALS TO PRE-K – FIRST GRADE

See cedarfort.com for more uplifting children's books.

EBOOK

CFI
AN IMPRINT OF CEDAR FORT, INC.

CEDAR FORT
Publishing & Media

WWW.CEDARFORT.COM
WWW.AUTHORTIFFANYTHOMAS.COM

LAMB BOOKS
Sight Reading

Jesus Loves Kids

LAMB
BOOKS
Sight Reading

N TESTAMENT STORIES

Jesus Loves Kids

written by Tiffany Thomas
illustrated by Nikki Casassa

CFI • An imprint of Cedar Fort, Inc. • Springville, Utah

HARD WORDS:

travel, blessing, heaven

PARENT TIP: Practice the "silent e" rul in words with and without the e (cut/cute, ma mate, bit/bite, rot/rote).

Jesus is travelling.

He is very tired.

Some people stop Jesus.

They want Him to bless their kids.

The Apostles tell them to go awa

They want Jesus to be able to rest.

But Jesus loves kids.

e tells the kids to come to Him.

He gives each kid a blessing.

e tells the Apostles to be like kids.

Then they can live
with God in Heaven.

The end.

ISBN 13: 978-1-4621-4403-7

Published by CFI, an imprint of Cedar Fort, Inc. • 2373 W. 700 S., Suite 100, Springville, UT 84663
Distributed by Cedar Fort, Inc., www.cedarfort.com

Library of Congress Control Number: 2022950658

Cover design and interior layout design by Shawnda T. Craig

Printed in China • Printed on acid-free paper
10 9 8 7 6 5 4 3 2 1

HELP your child read while also learning about the stories from the New Testament. Build your child's confidence in reading with the entire LAMB BOOKS series as they progress through each book!

MORE BOOK SETS AVAILABLE IN THE LAMB BOOKS SERIES

OLD TESTAMENT STORIES

FIRST GRADE READING LEVEL
APPEALS TO PRE-K – FIRST GRADE

See cedarfort.com for more uplifting children's books.

EBOOK

CFI
AN IMPRINT OF CEDAR FORT, INC.

CEDAR FORT Publishing & Media

WWW.CEDARFORT.COM

WWW.AUTHORTIFFANYTHOMAS.COM

The Rich Man

W TESTAMENT STORIES

LAMB
BOOKS
Sight Reading

The Rich Man

written by Tiffany Thomas
illustrated by Nikki Casassa

CFI • An imprint of Cedar Fort, Inc. • Springville, Utah

HARD WORDS:

rich, anything, obey

PARENT TIP: Explain that "q" almost always is paired with the letter "u" in a word.

A rich young man wants to go to heaven.

le asks Jesus what he needs to do.

Jesus tells him to obey his mom and dad.

Also not to lie, steal, or kill.

The young man says
he already obeys.

Then Jesus says he should sell all he has.

He should give the money to the poor.

The young man is sad and he leaves.

Jesus says he loves money more than God.

Those people cannot go to heaven.

We need to love God more than anything.

The end.

ISBN 13: 978-1-4621-4403-7

Published by CFI, an imprint of Cedar Fort, Inc. • 2373 W. 700 S., Suite 100, Springville, UT 84663
Distributed by Cedar Fort, Inc., www.cedarfort.com

Library of Congress Control Number: 2022950658

Cover design and interior layout design by Shawnda T. Craig

Printed in China • Printed on acid-free paper
10 9 8 7 6 5 4 3 2 1

HELP your child read while also learning about the stories from the New Testament. Build your child's confidence in reading with the entire LAMB BOOKS series as they progress through each book!

MORE BOOK SETS AVAILABLE IN THE LAMB BOOKS SERIES

OLD TESTAMENT STORIES

FIRST GRADE READING LEVEL
APPEALS TO PRE-K – FIRST GRADE

See cedarfort.com for more uplifting children's books.

EBOOK

CFI
AN IMPRINT OF CEDAR FORT, INC.

CEDAR FORT
Publishing & Media

WWW.CEDARFORT.COM
WWW.AUTHORTIFFANYTHOMAS.COM

Lazarus Lives Again

K

.W TESTAMENT STORIES

LAMB BOOKS

Sight Reading

Lazarus Lives Again

written by Tiffany Thomas
illustrated by Nikki Casassa

CFI • An imprint of Cedar Fort, Inc. • Springville, Utah

HARD WORDS:

Lazarus, tomb, alive

PARENT TIP: There are many double letters in this story: pretty, marry, all. Point out that your child does not have to say the letter two times.

This is Lazarus.
He is Jesus's friend.

His sisters are
Mary and Martha.

They love Jesus, too.

Lazarus gets sick and dies.

Jesus hears the sad news and comes to the women.

Martha says Jesus could have healed Lazarus.

Jesus tells her he will live again.

Martha says she believes and gets Mary.

Lazarus is inside a tomb.
Jesus goes to the tomb and prays

He tells Lazarus to come out.

Lazarus is alive again!

The end.

ISBN 13: 978-1-4621-4403-7

Published by CFI, an imprint of Cedar Fort, Inc. • 2373 W. 700 S., Suite 100, Springville, UT 84663
Distributed by Cedar Fort, Inc., www.cedarfort.com

Library of Congress Control Number: 2022950658

Cover design and interior layout design by Shawnda T. Craig

Printed in China • Printed on acid-free paper
10 9 8 7 6 5 4 3 2 1

HELP your child read while also learning about the stories from the New Testament. Build your child's confidence in reading with the entire LAMB BOOKS series as they progress through each book!

MORE BOOK SETS AVAILABLE IN THE LAMB BOOKS SERIES

OLD TESTAMENT STORIES

FIRST GRADE READING LEVEL
APPEALS TO PRE-K – FIRST GRADE

See cedarfort.com for more uplifting children's books.

CFI
AN IMPRINT OF CEDAR FORT, INC.
CEDAR FORT Publishing & Media
WWW.CEDARFORT.COM
WWW.AUTHORTIFFANYTHOMAS.COM

The Woman Gives All

LAMB
BOOKS
Sight Reading

ɔK

ɛW TESTAMENT STORIES

The Woman Gives All

written by Tiffany Thomas
illustrated by Nikki Casassa

CFI • An imprint of Cedar Fort, Inc. • Springville, Utah

HARD WORDS:

widow, tithing, owned

PARENT TIP: Point out that two, too, and to are three different words that sound the same, but each different meaning has a different spelling.

This is a poor widow.

Her husband died.

She does not have much money.

In the temple, people pay tithing.

They put the tithing in a box.

Rich men come and give a lot of money.

The woman
gives only
two mites.

Jesus says
she gave all
the money
she had.

She has no more money left.

Jesus says she gave more
to God than the rich did.

She will be blessed.

The end.

ISBN 13: 978-1-4621-4403-7

Published by CFI, an imprint of Cedar Fort, Inc. • 2373 W. 700 S., Suite 100, Springville, UT 84663
Distributed by Cedar Fort, Inc., www.cedarfort.com

Library of Congress Control Number: 2022950658

Cover design and interior layout design by Shawnda T. Craig

Printed in China • Printed on acid-free paper
10 9 8 7 6 5 4 3 2 1

HELP your child read while also learning about the stories from the New Testament. Build your child's confidence in reading with the entire LAMB BOOKS series as they progress through each book!

MORE BOOK SETS AVAILABLE IN THE LAMB BOOKS SERIES

OLD TESTAMENT STORIES

FIRST GRADE READING LEVEL
APPEALS TO PRE-K – FIRST GRADE

See cedarfort.com for more uplifting children's books.

CFI
AN IMPRINT OF CEDAR FORT, INC.
CEDAR FORT Publishing & Media
WWW.CEDARFORT.COM
WWW.AUTHORTIFFANYTHOMAS.COM

The Ten Women

K

EW TESTAMENT STORIES

LAMB
BOOKS
Sight Reading

The Ten Women

written by Tiffany Thomas
illustrated by Nikki Casassa

CFI • An imprint of Cedar Fort, Inc. • Springville, Utah

HARD WORDS:
wedding, oil, night

PARENT TIP: The illustrations on each page will help your child understand and learn the words.

Jesus tells a story about when He comes again.

Ten women wait for a wedding at night.

They have lamps with oil for light.

Five wise women have extra oil.

Five foolish women do not.
Their lamps burn out.

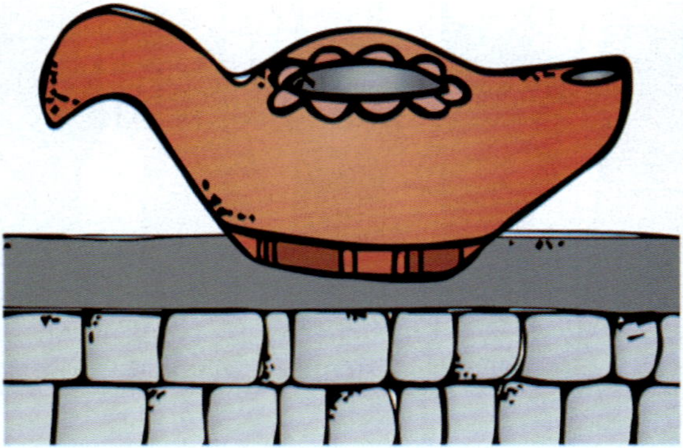

They ask the five wise to share, but there isn't enough.

The five foolish women
have to look for oil.

It takes them too long.
They miss the wedding.

The wedding is the Second Coming

The oil is our good deeds.

We must watch and
be ready for Jesus.

The end.

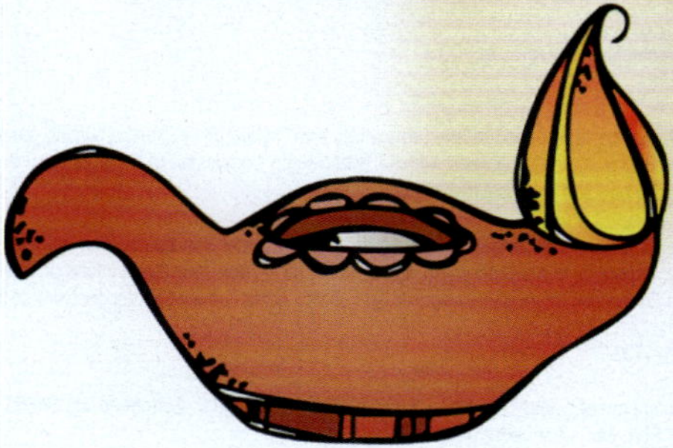

ISBN 13: 978-1-4621-4403-7

Published by CFI, an imprint of Cedar Fort, Inc. • 2373 W. 700 S., Suite 100, Springville, UT 84663
Distributed by Cedar Fort, Inc., www.cedarfort.com

Library of Congress Control Number: 2022950658

Cover design and interior layout design by Shawnda T. Craig

Printed in China • Printed on acid-free paper
10 9 8 7 6 5 4 3 2 1

HELP your child read while also learning about the stories from the New Testament. Build your child's confidence in reading with the entire LAMB BOOKS series as they progress through each book!

MORE BOOK SETS AVAILABLE IN THE LAMB BOOKS SERIES

OLD TESTAMENT STORIES

FIRST GRADE READING LEVEL
APPEALS TO PRE-K – FIRST GRADE

See cedarfort.com for more uplifting children's books.

ALSO AVAILABLE AS AN EBOOK

CFI
AN IMPRINT OF CEDAR FORT, INC.

CEDAR FORT
Publishing & Media

WWW.CEDARFORT.COM
WWW.AUTHORTIFFANYTHOMAS.COM

Jesus Gives the Sacrament

OK

EW TESTAMENT STORIES

LAMB
BOOKS
Sight Reading

Jesus Gives the Sacrament

written by Tiffany Thomas
illustrated by Nikki Casassa

CFI • An imprint of Cedar Fort, Inc. • Springville, Utah

HARD WORDS:

feast, sacrament, branch

PARENT TIP: Point out spaces between words and all of the different punctuation marks.

Jesus has a feast with the Apostle

Jesus says a special prayer.

He gives them bread and wine.

The bread is for His body.

The wine is for His blood.

He tells them to remember Him.

Jesus says bad
men will kill Him.

He says one of the Apostles will help the bad men.

Jesus says to serve others and pra

He tells them He is a vine,
and they are branches.

They must hold tight to Him.

The end.

ISBN 13: 978-1-4621-4403-7

Published by CFI, an imprint of Cedar Fort, Inc. • 2373 W. 700 S., Suite 100, Springville, UT 84663
Distributed by Cedar Fort, Inc., www.cedarfort.com

Library of Congress Control Number: 2022950658

Cover design and interior layout design by Shawnda T. Craig

Printed in China • Printed on acid-free paper
10 9 8 7 6 5 4 3 2 1

HELP your child read while also learning about the stories from the New Testament. Build your child's confidence in reading with the entire LAMB BOOKS series as they progress through each book!

MORE BOOK SETS AVAILABLE IN THE LAMB BOOKS SERIES

OLD TESTAMENT STORIES

FIRST GRADE READING LEVEL
APPEALS TO PRE-K – FIRST GRADE

See cedarfort.com for more uplifting children's books.

ALSO AVAILABLE AS AN EBOOK

CFI AN IMPRINT OF CEDAR FORT, INC.

CEDAR FORT Publishing & Media

WWW.CEDARFORT.COM

WWW.AUTHORTIFFANYTHOMAS.COM

Jesus Suffers in the Garden

LAMB
BOOKS
Sight Reading

W TESTAMENT STORIES

Jesus Suffers in the Garden

written by Tiffany Thomas
illustrated by Nikki Casassa

CFI • An imprint of Cedar Fort, Inc. • Springville, Utah

HARD WORDS:

garden, gethsemane, wrong

PARENT TIP: Explain that "some" does not use the silent e rule. Another exception is "come."

This is the Garden of Gethsemane

Jesus goes there with
Peter, James, and John.

Jesus prays.

Peter, James, and John fall asleep.

Jesus shakes because He is in pain

He suffers for our sins.

An angel comes to give Him strengt

Jesus bleeds all over His body.

He feels the pain of all
of our wrong choices.

Now He can forgive us if we repent.

Jesus wakes up Peter, James, and John.

The end.

ISBN 13: 978-1-4621-4403-7

Published by CFI, an imprint of Cedar Fort, Inc. • 2373 W. 700 S., Suite 100, Springville, UT 84663
Distributed by Cedar Fort, Inc., www.cedarfort.com

Library of Congress Control Number: 2022950658

Cover design and interior layout design by Shawnda T. Craig

Printed in China • Printed on acid-free paper
10 9 8 7 6 5 4 3 2 1

HELP your child read while also learning about the stories from the New Testament. Build your child's confidence in reading with the entire LAMB BOOKS series as they progress through each book!

MORE BOOK SETS AVAILABLE IN THE LAMB BOOKS SERIES

OLD TESTAMENT STORIES

FIRST GRADE READING LEVEL
APPEALS TO PRE-K – FIRST GRADE

See cedarfort.com for more uplifting children's books.

ALSO AVAILABLE AS AN EBOOK

CFI
AN IMPRINT OF CEDAR FORT, INC.

CEDAR FORT
Publishing & Media

WWW.CEDARFORT.COM
WWW.AUTHORTIFFANYTHOMAS.COM

Jesus Dies on the Cross

K

EW TESTAMENT STORIES

LAMB BOOKS

Sight Reading

Jesus Dies on the Cross

written by Tiffany Thomas
illustrated by Nikki Casassa

CFI • An imprint of Cedar Fort, Inc. • Springville, Utah

HARD WORDS:

whip, cross, soldier

PARENT TIP: "sh" can be difficult for younger children to pronounce. Allow them to develop at their own pace for a little bit.

The Apostle Judas comes with bad men.

They take Jesus away
to the leaders.

He tells them
He is the
Son of God.

The leaders all want to kill Jesus.

They beat Jesus with whips and hurt Him.

The soldiers take Jesus to a hill.

Jesus carries His own cross.

They nail His hands, wrists, and feet to it.

Jesus prays for the soldiers to be forgiven.

s mother Mary is there. She is sad.

Jesus dies, and the earth shakes.

The end.

ISBN 13: 978-1-4621-4403-7

Published by CFI, an imprint of Cedar Fort, Inc. • 2373 W. 700 S., Suite 100, Springville, UT 84663
Distributed by Cedar Fort, Inc., www.cedarfort.com

Library of Congress Control Number: 2022950658

Cover design and interior layout design by Shawnda T. Craig

Printed in China • Printed on acid-free paper
10 9 8 7 6 5 4 3 2 1

HELP your child read while also learning about the stories from the New Testament. Build your child's confidence in reading with the entire LAMB BOOKS series as they progress through each book!

MORE BOOK SETS AVAILABLE IN THE LAMB BOOKS SERIES

OLD TESTAMENT STORIES

FIRST GRADE READING LEVEL
APPEALS TO PRE-K – FIRST GRADE

See cedarfort.com for more uplifting children's books.

EBOOK
CFI
AN IMPRINT OF CEDAR FORT, INC.
CEDAR FORT
Publishing & Media
WWW.CEDARFORT.COM
WWW.AUTHORTIFFANYTHOMAS.COM

LAMB BOOKS
Sight Reading

Jesus Is Risen

OOK
25

NEW TESTAMENT STORIES

LAMB
BOOKS
Sight Reading

Jesus Is Risen

written by Tiffany Thomas
illustrated by Nikki Casassa

CFI • An imprint of Cedar Fort, Inc. • Springville, Utah

HARD WORDS:

tomb, empty, risen

PARENT TIP: Words that begin with "wh" can be tricky. Instead of sounding them out, have them become sight words to memorize.

Jesus's friends take His body from the cross.

They put Him in a tomb.

Three days later, angels take the stone off of the tomb.

Jesus's friend Mary
comes to the tomb.

It is empty! Jesus is not there.

She runs to tell Peter and John.

They are sad and think people stole Jesus's body. Peter and John leave.

Mary stays at the tomb and cries.

Mary hears
a kind voice
ask her why
she is crying.

It is Jesus! He is alive again!

He tells her to go tell the Apostles He is risen.

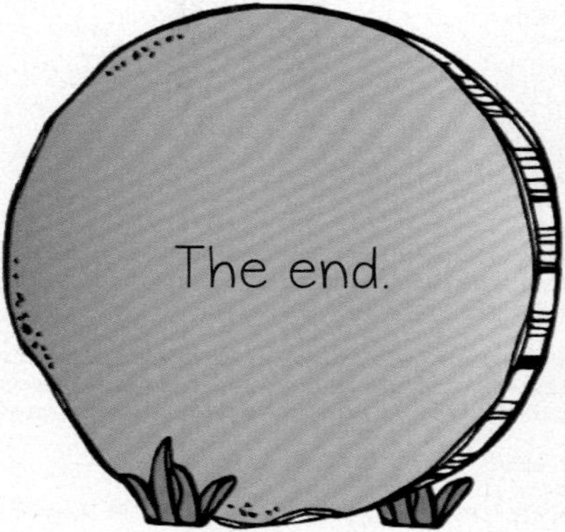

The end.

ISBN 13: 978-1-4621-4403-7

Published by CFI, an imprint of Cedar Fort, Inc. • 2373 W. 700 S., Suite 100, Springville, UT 84663
Distributed by Cedar Fort, Inc., www.cedarfort.com

Library of Congress Control Number: 2022950658

Cover design and interior layout design by Shawnda T. Craig

Printed in China • Printed on acid-free paper
10 9 8 7 6 5 4 3 2 1

HELP your child read while also learning about the stories from the New Testament. Build your child's confidence in reading with the entire LAMB BOOKS series as they progress through each book!

MORE BOOK SETS AVAILABLE IN THE LAMB BOOKS SERIES

OLD TESTAMENT STORIES

FIRST GRADE READING LEVEL
APPEALS TO PRE-K – FIRST GRADE

See cedarfort.com for more uplifting children's books.

ALSO AVAILABLE AS AN EBOOK

CFI
AN IMPRINT OF CEDAR FORT, INC

CEDAR FORT Publishing & Media

WWW.CEDARFORT.COM
WWW.AUTHORTIFFANYTHOMAS.COM

LAM
BOOKS
Sight Reading